Unicorns

New and future titles in the series include:

Alien Abductions

Angels

The Bermuda Triangle

The Curse of King Tut

ESP

Extinction of the Dinosaurs

Haunted Houses

Unicorns

UFOs

Vampires

Witches

The Mystery Library

Unicorns

Patricia D. Netzley

Lucent Books, Inc.
P.O. Box 289011, San Diego, California

For Raymond, Matthew, Sarah, and Jacob

Library of Congress Cataloging-in-Publication Data

Netzley, Patricia D.
  Unicorns / by Patricia D. Netzley.
    p. cm. — (The mystery library)
Includes bibliographical references and index.
Summary: Discusses this mythical beast and the roles it has
played in legend, religion, and medieval medicine, as well as
man's efforts to prove its existence.
  ISBN 1-56006-687-3 (hardcover : alk. paper)
  1. Unicorns—Juvenile literature. [1. Unicorns.] I. Title. II.
Mystery library (Lucent Books)
  GR830.U6 N47 2001
  398'.469—dc21

                                                      00-008640

Copyright 2001 by Lucent Books, Inc.
P.O. Box 289011, San Diego, California 92198-9011

Printed in the U.S.A.

Contents

Foreword

In Shakespeare's immortal play, *Hamlet*, the young Danish aristocrat Horatio has clearly been astonished and disconcerted by his encounter with a ghost-like apparition on the castle battlements. "There are more things in heaven and earth," his friend Hamlet assures him, "than are dreamt of in your philosophy."

Many people today would readily agree with Hamlet that the world and the vast universe surrounding it are teeming with wonders and oddities that remain largely outside the realm of present human knowledge or understanding. How did the universe begin? What caused the dinosaurs to become extinct? Was the lost continent of Atlantis a real place or merely legendary? Does a monstrous creature lurk beneath the surface of Scotland's Loch Ness? These are only a few of the intriguing questions that remain unanswered, despite the many great strides made by science in recent centuries.

Lucent Books' Mystery Library series is dedicated to exploring these and other perplexing, sometimes bizarre, and often disturbing or frightening wonders. Each volume in the series presents the best-known tales, incidents, and evidence surrounding the topic in question. Also included are the opinions and theories of scientists and other experts who have attempted to unravel and solve the ongoing mystery. And supplementing this information is a fulsome list of sources for further reading, providing the reader with the means to pursue the topic further.

The Mystery Library will satisfy every young reader's fascination for the unexplained. As one of history's greatest scientists, physicist Albert Einstein, put it:

> The most beautiful thing we can experience is the mysterious. It is the source of all true art and science. He to whom this emotion is a stranger, who can no longer wonder and stand rapt in awe, is as good as dead: his eyes are closed.

Introduction

An Enduring Figure

References to unicorns can be found in various cultures throughout history.

A sk people today to describe a unicorn, and most will tell of a snow-white horse with a long white mane and tail and a single horn growing out of its forehead. Yet at various times and places in history, the creature has been portrayed as white, tan, red, or a mixture of colors. Its body has been said to be similar to that of an antelope, a horse, an ox, a deer, or sometimes even a mixture of several animals; one Chinese legend features a unicorn with the body of a deer and the head of a wolf.

The one constant in all of these descriptions is the unicorn's single horn. In fact, the name *unicorn* is from the Latin word *unicornis*, which means "single-horned." The single horn, however, is where the similarities end. Cultures throughout history have disagreed about everything from the unicorn's symbolic significance to whether the animal ever existed at all. And it is this disagreement that makes the unicorn one of mankind's greatest mysteries.

Fact or Fiction?

Most modern researchers agree that the reason for these discrepancies lies in the fact that the unicorn is a mythological beast, created by storytellers from different parts of the world who each imagined the animal somewhat differently. Many scholars believe that these storytellers got the idea for a fictional unicorn by seeing real single-horned animals like the rhinoceros; others, however, think that unicorns were not the product of storytelling but of rumor, as reports of animals like the rhinoceros were misinterpreted. Still other scholars believe that there might actually have been a real unicorn, a unique single-horned beast that is now extinct.

This fifteenth-century tapestry is just one example of humanity's long-held belief in unicorns.

Regardless, as scholars debate the source of unicorn stories, popular culture employs the unicorn as a symbol whose meaning has changed over time. Today the unicorn is typically associated with little girls, appearing on such items as pillows, sheets, and toy chests as a symbol of childhood. But in earlier times it represented not only purity and goodness but also various religious beliefs. And because the unicorn was associated with religion, it was also connected to faith.

Perhaps that is why the unicorn has been such an enduring figure over the centuries. Believing in it has become a test of faith in the mysterious and wondrous. As Nigel Suckling says in his *The Book of the Unicorn,*

> It hardly matters whether Unicorns are or ever have been real, enjoyable though it would be to prove it.

What really counts is the supposed nature of the beast, because it tells us something about ourselves. Just as the world divides between those who love, loathe or are indifferent to cats and dogs, so one's response to Unicorns says something about the person.[1]

Chapter 1

What Is the Unicorn?

Throughout history, descriptions of unicorns have appeared in two distinct forms: stories about mythological beasts and reports of real living creatures. The mythological stories originated in Asia, and reports of living unicorns came first from ancient Greeks and Romans and later from medieval European scholars. Interestingly, although Eastern and Western sources presented the unicorn in different ways, there were many similarities in their accounts.

A Beast of Many Parts

In many of the mythological stories, the unicorn is described as a unique beast sharing the characteristics of several different animals. The Chinese unicorn, for example, had the head and body of a stag, the legs of a horse, and a twelve-foot-long single horn on its forehead. Believed to live in the heavens, it was thought to have the same brilliant array of colors as the sky at various times of day: blue, red, yellow, white, and black.

The mythological Japanese unicorn was also an amalgamation of many animals. It was sometimes said to have a bull's body, but other times it was said to resemble a deer or goat. In either case, its eyes were so fearsome that they could frighten a person into immobility. Both the Chinese

Myths about unicorns can be found in many Asian cultures. This sixteenth-century silk badge depicts one Chinese version of the unicorn.

and the Japanese unicorns had a straight, smooth, pointed horn, although descriptions of its length differed.

Western writers also sometimes told of a unicorn that was a combination of many different animals. For example, Pliny the Elder (also known as Gaius Plinius Secundus), a Roman naturalist who lived from approximately A.D. 23 to 79 produced an encyclopedia entitled *Historia naturalis*, in which he writes,

> The . . . Indians [of India] hunt an exceedingly wild beast called the monoceros [the Greek word for *unicorn*], which has a stag's head, elephant's feet, and a boar's tail, the rest of its body being like that of a horse. It makes a deep lowing noise, and one black horn two cubits long [about three feet] projects from the middle of its forehead. This animal, they say, cannot be taken alive.[2]

A Real Creature

Whereas the Chinese and Japanese thought of the unicorn as a mythological beast, Pliny believed that he was describing a real creature, one that lived on Earth rather than in heaven. Therefore, his unicorn was not brilliantly colored but appeared as any other animal, with a black horn and perhaps a gray or tan body. In fact, Pliny's description is similar to that of the rhinoceros, an animal that was often exhibited in the Roman circuses of his time. In writing about the unicorn—which Pliny himself admitted he had never seen—the scholar drew on what he knew about in nature.

This was also the case for the Roman scholar Aelianus (A.D. 170–235), whose description of the unicorn was similar to Pliny's. In his book *De natura animalium*, Aelianus writes,

> They say that there are mountains in the innermost regions of India inaccessible to men, and full of wild beasts. . . . Among them they enumerate the unicorn, which they call cartazonon, and say that it reaches the size of a horse of mature age, possesses a mane and reddish yellow hair, and that it excels in swiftness through the excellence of its feet and of its whole body. Like the elephant, it has inarticulate feet, and it has a boar's tail; one black horn projects between the eyebrows, not awkwardly, but with a certain natural twist, and terminating in a sharp point.[3]

Roman scholar Pliny the Elder believed unicorns were real creatures.

Greek Scholars

Like Pliny, Aelianus had never seen a unicorn himself. But both men believed in the existence of unicorns largely because of descriptions provided by ancient Greek scholars, who were the first people to write about real living unicorns. The first ancient Greek to describe the unicorn was Ctesias, a physician and historian who had heard about the animal while he was living in Persia in the late fifth century. The Persians had long told of a one-horned donkey whose native habitat was India. Therefore, when Ctesias wrote a book about India, *Indica*, he reported,

Even though he had never seen one, Greek scholar Aristotle included descriptions of unicorns in his writings.

Among the Indians . . . there are wild asses which are as large as horses, some being even larger. Their heads are of a dark red colour, their eyes blue, and the rest of their body white. They have a horn on their forehead, a cubit in length [about eighteen inches]. . . . This horn for about two palm-breadths upwards from the base is of the purest white, where it tapers to a sharp point of a flaming crimson, and, in the middle, is black[4]

Had Ctesias's account been the only one of its kind, the unicorn might have been considered a fictional creature from its first appearance in Western literature. However, several other notable Greek scholars also wrote about the creature as if it were a real being. One of the most prominent was Aristotle, a philosopher who lived from approximately 384–322 B.C. In his work *Historia animalium*, Aristotle attempted to categorize the known animals of his time, and among these he included two single-horned animals: an oryx and an Indian ass. Aristotle had never seen either of these two types of unicorns; in fact, although both the oryx and the Indian ass actually exist, neither of them has a single horn. The Indian ass has no horns, and the oryx has two. Nonetheless, most ancient Greeks accepted Aristotle's comments as accurate because he was a highly respected scholar—so respected that, according to Joe Nigg in his book *Wonder Beasts*, Aristotle's inclusion of unicorns in his *Historia animalium* was "one reason people believed in the unicorn for so long."[5]

Another influential Greek was a biographer named Philostratus the Athenian. In approximately A.D. 220, he wrote about a traveler, Apollonius of Tyana (in Greece), who had seen a unicorn while in India. Actually, Apollonius himself never wrote about seeing a unicorn, although historians do know that he traveled from

Greece to India in the first century A.D. But because Philostratus stated that Apollonius had seen a unicorn, most people believed it. In Appollonius's biography, Philostratus writes, "And they say that wild asses are also to be captured in these marshes, and these creatures have a horn upon the forehead, with which they butt like a bull and make a noble fight of it. . . . And Apollonius says that he saw this animal, and admired its natural features."[6]

Various Habitats

Philostratus was one of many Western scholars who placed the unicorn's habitat in India. Modern scholars speculate that this location was chosen because of the many mythological unicorn stories coming out of the Far East. As travelers carried these stories west, scholars suggest, they were mistaken for fact rather than fiction.

The Far East might also have been chosen because it was, to ancient and medieval scholars, as exotic and mysterious as the unicorn itself. Surely the unicorn had to live in a faraway land, such scholars argued, since it had never been exhibited in Roman circuses. This same argument was used to place the unicorn in the New World after America was discovered in 1492. At that time, many people suggested that unicorns would eventually be found on the American continent.

In fact, as explorers ventured into new lands they brought back stories of unicorns. For example, the thirteenth-century Italian explorer Marco Polo said that he saw unicorns on an Indonesian island now called Sumatra. In his book *Travels*, he says,

> There are wild elephants in the country, and numerous unicorns, which are very nearly as big. They have hair like that of a buffalo, feet like those of an elephant, and very thick. They do no mischief,

however, with the horn, but with the tongue alone; for this is covered all over with long and strong prickles (and when savage with any one they crush him under their knees and then rasp him with their tongue). The head resembles that of a wild boar, and they carry it ever bent towards the ground. They delight much to abide in mire and mud. 'Tis a passing ugly beast to look upon.[7]

Marco Polo's description of unicorns in the Far East led to continued speculation that unicorns lived in exotic and mysterious places.

An Elusive Animal

But even as explorers reported unicorns in exotic places, other people said the beasts lived closer to home. Such people believed that the unicorn was rarely seen because it was an elusive and solitary animal, not because it was in another land. According to this view, the most likely habitat for the unicorn was a thick forest, a vast desert, or a high mountaintop. For example, Julius Caesar, who lived from approximately 100–44 B.C. and was dictator of Rome from 46–44 B.C., thought that the unicorn lived in European woods. In his book *The Gallic Wars,* he writes, "There is [in the Hercynian forest in Germany] an ox, shaped like a stag, from the middle of whose forehead, between the ears, stands a single horn, taller and straighter than the horns we know."[8]

In the sixteenth century, Lodovico de Varthema, also known as Lewis Vartoman, said that the unicorn also lived in Middle Eastern deserts. In fact, he claimed to have seen one in the holy city of Mecca. In his book *Itinerario* (*Travels*) he writes,

Roman general Julius Caesar believed unicorns lived in European forests.

In another part of the . . . temple is an enclosed place in which there are two live unicorns, and these are shown as very remarkable objects, which they certainly are. I will tell you how they are made. The elder is formed like a colt of thirty months old, and he has a horn in the forehead, which horn is about three *braccia* [arm lengths] in length. The other unicorn is like a colt of one year old, and he has a horn of about four *palmi* [hand's lengths] long. The colour of the said animal resembles that of a dark bay horse, and his head resembles that of a stag; his neck is not very long, and he has some thin and short hair which hangs on one side; his legs are slender and lean like those of a goat; the foot is a little cloven in the fore part, and long and goat-like, and there are some hairs on the hind part of the said legs. Truly this monster must be a very fierce and solitary animal.[9]

A Fierce Creature

By the Middle Ages, almost everyone who described a unicorn mentioned its fierceness. The animal was said to be naturally gentle but willing to fight to the death to avoid capture. This quality was first mentioned by ancient scholars. For instance, in his book *De natura animalium*, Aelianus explains that unicorns had to be captured while young if they were going to be captured at all, because once mature they would never be taken alive:

> [The unicorn] is said to be gentle to other beasts approaching it, but to fight with its fellows. . . . It frequents desert regions and wanders alone and solitary. . . . They say that the young, while still of tender age, are carried to the King of the Prasians [Persians] for exhibition of their strength, and exposed in combats on festivals; for no one remembers them to have been captured of mature age.[10]

Ctesias also wrote of the unicorn's fierceness. Passing on information provided to him by the Persians, he told of unicorn hunts in India during which unicorns were killed for their horns. Ctesias reported that the animals not only fought to the death but were also so swift that they could not be overtaken by a man on horseback:

> On first starting [the unicorn] scampers off somewhat leisurely, but the longer it runs, it gallops faster and faster till the pace becomes most furious.

These animals therefore can only be caught at one particular time—that is when they lead out their little foals to the pastures in which they roam. They are then hemmed in on all sides by a vast number of hunters mounted on horseback, and being unwilling to escape while leaving their young to perish, stand their ground and fight, and by butting with their horns and kicking and biting kill many horses and men. But they are in the end taken, pierced to death with arrows and spears, for to take them alive is in no way possible. Their flesh being bitter is unfit for food, and they are hunted merely for the sake of their horns and their huckle-bones.[11]

The Maiden and the Unicorn

Stories of unicorn hunts became extremely popular during the Middle Ages, and many tapestries depicted unicorns fighting to the death. Sometime during this period, the standard color for the unicorn became white, perhaps to reflect its purity and goodness. Also during this period, a new feature was added to unicorn stories: It was said that the presence of a young maiden would make a unicorn docile. According to medieval writers, a unicorn was so attracted to maidens that, when it saw one, it would lay its head in her lap. This would enable a hunter, approaching stealthily, to kill or capture the unicorn with ease.

Some medieval people said that unicorns recognized a maiden by her scent, but others believed that the unicorn could be tricked into believing that a male hunter was a maiden if he dressed in women's clothes. A few writers advised hunters to use a maiden as unicorn bait, even tying her to a tree if she would not cooperate freely. In the early twelfth century, a nun in Bingen, Germany, the Abbess Hildegarde, advised using a group of maidens to capture a unicorn:

This sixteenth-century painting depicts the medieval belief that unicorns would become docile in the presence of young maidens.

On the day of the hunt, men, women, and young girls pursue the unicorn. Then the girls separate from the others and go off to gather flowers in a meadow. The unicorn, upon seeing the girls, stops at once, crouches on his hind legs in the tall grass, and watches them for a long time. He falls in love with the girls, for he sees that they are gentle and kind. But while he is gazing at them, the men slay the unicorn and cut off its horn.[12]

Modern scholars are unsure why medieval writers began to talk about using maidens to capture unicorns. Professor Leo Wiener of Harvard University believes that these stories have their origin in a mistake. During the

Middle Ages, a collection of animal stories called the *Physiologus* featured a tale about the unicorn. There is no mention of a maiden in this story, but in another tale in the collection, an antelope is caught in a trap made of twigs. The word for *twigs* in Latin, the language of the *Physiologus*, is *virge*. The word for an unmarried maiden, or virgin, is *virgo*. Wiener therefore suggests that someone either misread or miswrote the word for twigs, and that the antelope and unicorn stories were confused with one another.

Were They Real?

Regardless of how the maiden/unicorn stories developed, no medieval author claimed to have witnessed a unicorn capture. In fact, most medieval reports of unicorn sightings were based on hearsay—stories reported second-, third-, or even fourth-hand. Only a few people insisted that they themselves had seen a unicorn.

Consequently modern scholars have debated whether there ever was a real unicorn to inspire these stories. Most say there was not, believing that the idea of a living unicorn came from myth. For example, scholar Odell Shepard says that Ctesias's description of the unicorn—on which many subsequent unicorn accounts seem to have been based—resulted from a poor memory and the confusion of several stories. In his book *The Lore of the Unicorn*, Shepard states, "Evidently, Ctesias is describing at least two different animals at once, and it is as though a child, having read descriptions of the lion and the camel, should combine them into a [beast] vaguely like both but exactly similar to neither."[13] Shepard thinks that Ctesias's unicorn was actually three animals mixed together: an Indian rhinoceros, a Persian wild ass, and a Tibetan antelope.

Shepard further believes that firsthand unicorn accounts, such as that of Marco Polo, were actually describing rhinoceroses rather than unicorns. Shepard even thinks that the maiden/unicorn stories came from a rhinoceros story told around campfires by ancient Ethiopian hunters. In this tale, a female monkey is used to catch a rhinoceros by rubbing the animal's stomach to calm it; Shepard argues that over many retellings, the monkey became a maiden. Shepard summarizes the tale:

> The hunters go into the province of Goyame, which is at the base of the Mountains of the Moon whence the Nile springs, for there alone, in all Africa, are these beasts to be found. When they learn that one is near at hand they load their muskets and they take a female monkey which they have trained for this kind of hunting, and they

Many scholars believe that the ancient accounts of unicorns were actually descriptions of rhinoceroses.

bring her to the place. She begins at once to run about looking for the rhinoceros, and when she sees him she leaps here and there and dances as she goes toward him, playing a thousand monkey-tricks. He is much delighted in watching this entertainment, so that she is able to approach. . . . Then she begins scratching and rubbing his hide, and this gives him keen pleasure. At last, jumping to the ground again, she starts to rub his belly, and then the rhinoceros is so overcome with ecstasy that he stretches himself out at length upon the ground. At this point the hunters, who have been hidden all the while in some safe place, come up with their cross-bows or muskets and shoot him.[14]

But in going so far to argue that all ancient and medieval unicorn references were really rhinoceros references, Odell dismisses reports like Lodovico de Varthema's, which clearly describes a horselike unicorn, as flights of fancy inspired by Eastern myths. Other people, however, argue that such reports must be taken more seriously. They suggest that Varthema could have seen a real unicorn, and that this unicorn—not a rhinoceros but a horse with a horn—could have been the inspiration for Eastern unicorn myths. Given the similarities among Eastern and Western descriptions of unicorns, surely this possibility cannot be entirely discounted. Perhaps there truly was a living unicorn whose image was familiar to mythmakers and storytellers—an image that still persists today, even if the animal does not.

Chapter 2

A Symbolic Beast

Whereas ancient and medieval scholars were concerned with determining what the unicorn looked and acted like and where it lived, storytellers throughout history have been more interested in using the unicorn as a symbol. To some of these people, the unicorn represents elements of the gods; to others, it represents elements of humanity.

Good Fortune

To the Chinese, the unicorn is a symbol of good fortune—or, as one anonymous ninth-century Chinese poet put it, "a supernatural being and of auspicious [favorable] omen."[15] Ancient Chinese writings say that the unicorn—called the *ki-lin* (also spelled *Ch'I-lin* or *Chhi Lin*)—lived in the heavens but first appeared on Earth in 2697 B.C. as a sign that the reign of Emperor Hwang-ti would be beneficial to China. The unicorn was also said to appear on Earth to herald the birth of an unusually great and/or wise man. According to one folktale, the unicorn visited the mother of Confucius, a great Chinese philosopher, before his conception to foretell his birth.

Because of such stories, the Chinese consider the unicorn particularly lucky in regard to a child's birth. Odell Shepard explains:

In Chinese culture, uni-corns are seen as symbols of good fortune.

Events of this sort [i.e., the appearance of the unicorn before the birth of Confucius] have occurred so many times and the prophecy has always been so unerring that pictures of the uni-corn are now pinned or pasted in the women's quarters of millions of Chinese houses in the hope that they may exert pre-natal influence and induce the birth of great men, or at least of boys rather than of girls. They are also affixed to the red chair in which the bride is borne to her hus-band's house, and the gods that oversee the distri-bution of desirable babies are often depicted rid-ing the ki-lin. To say of any man that a ki-lin appeared at the time of his birth is the highest form of flattery.[16]

The Chinese further believe that when the unicorn is not acting as a bearer of good fortune, it is acting as a god in charge of all the animals of the earth. Ancient Chinese legends say that the unicorn is one of four immortal beings who rule the heavens as well as various aspects of the earth. The other three beings are the phoenix (a mythical bird with brilliant plumage), the turtle, and the dragon. The unicorn governs land animals, the phoenix governs birds, the turtle governs all sea creatures, and the dragon governs the wind and weather. In addition, each of the four immortal beings represents a different element: the unicorn, earth; the phoenix, fire; the dragon, air; and the turtle, water.

But although the Chinese unicorn is associated with the gods, it is also said to have humanlike qualities. In fact, the unicorn represents ideal human behavior, a symbol of the best attributes every human should have. Therefore, the Chinese unicorn is said to be respectful to his parents and reverential to his ancestors. He is gentle, kind, and good, never using his horn as a weapon. He speaks out against evil and does not allow himself to be exploited; hunters do not take his horn, nor is he exhibited for sport in any arena. In fact, he avoids all human contact unless he is on a mission of the gods, remaining in heaven until he is needed to bring good fortune to the Chinese people.

Tools of Mankind

To the Japanese, the unicorn is also associated with the gods, but it is primarily a symbol of justice. In Japanese stories the unicorn is said to have the ability to look into a man's soul and determine his guilt or innocence. In many of these stories, the unicorn is brought into a courtroom to judge the guilt of a man accused of a crime. The unicorn's presence is not requested for ordinary legal cases only those involving extreme offenses and difficult judgments. If the unicorn looks into the defendant's eyes and sees that he is guilty, the creature stabs the man in the heart with its horn, killing him.

Like the Japanese, Chinese legends also tell of a beast that was used to judge a person's guilt or innocence. However, it is uncertain whether this beast is a *ki-lin*. Some accounts suggest that it was a ram or a goat born with only one horn. Moreover, in these legends, when the animal judged a man guilty, it did not execute him. Instead, the condemned was executed by court officials.

To the ancient Arabians, however, the unicorn did not symbolize judgment or fortune. Instead, it represented a challenge to manhood. Arabian stories tell of a fierce unicorn

This thirteenth-century manuscript page shows a karkadann, *or Arabian unicorn. The ancient Arabians believed that the unicorn was a continual challenge to manhood.*

called the *karkadann* that was given to attacking men and animals simply because they invaded its territory. Big enough to impale and lift an elephant on its horn, it was said to be the most challenging prey for any hunter. Many stories were told of men who proved their manhood by hunting a *karkadann*. In one such story, a young man goes off alone to find and kill a *karkadann* and never returns. His twin brother then goes looking for him and discovers the young man trapped on a *karkadann's* horn, his thigh pierced straight through. The twin summons the courage to attack and kills the *karkadann* with a knife, thereby saving his brother's life.

The Celestial Battle

The ancient Mesopotamians, however, used the unicorn to symbolize a different kind of battle—one that took place in the heavens rather than on Earth. They left behind numerous artifacts bearing the image of the unicorn fighting with a lion, as Elizabeth Pool describes in her book *The Unicorn Was There:*

> On walls and robes, jewelry, boxes, and seals, the Mesopotamian lion relentlessly pursues his foe. Sometimes the unicorn halts. He lowers his horn and bends one knee as if both in challenge and greeting. The lion menaces, rearing up on his hind legs and spreading his paws, but he does not attack until the unicorn is once more in flight. Then the lion leaps, pinioning his prey. The unicorn surrenders—but he is not brought down and though his wounds are great they are never mortal.[17]

Pool and other modern scholars believe that, to the ancient Mesopotamians, the lion—a masculine creature with a round, fiery mane—represented the sun while the unicorn—a feminine creature with a crescent-shaped white horn—represented the moon. Therefore, the battle between the unicorn and the lion was representative of the

The ancient Mesopotamians believed that the unicorn repre-sented the moon in the ongoing celestial battle between the sun and moon.

celestial drama that the ancient Mesopotamians saw each day in the sky. Pool explains:

> The unicorn-moon challenges the lion-sun and there is strife in the sky until, weary and wounded, the unicorn sinks from sight. . . . Time passes and the nights are dark, but presently the bright horn re-appears. The uni-corn is swift. He races across the sky, now low on the horizon, now high among the stars. Pursued by the sun, he assumes disguises—altering the shape of his horn, rolling into a silver ball—but never is the end in doubt.

The lion will win. And yet, so long as the unicorn is there to challenge again, no victory can be complete.[18]

A National Symbol

The battle between lion and unicorn has also been depicted in many medieval works of literature and art. In one popular story, the unicorn charges at the lion, who quickly steps aside. Unable to stop his charge, the unicorn gets his horn stuck in a tree, and the lion eats him. This story was used to show that even the fiercest fighter—represented by the unicorn—can be vanquished by his own foolhardiness.

To medieval people, the unicorn also symbolized a worthy opponent in battles, eventually evolving to represent the Scottish people specifically. No one knows when or why the unicorn was first adopted as the symbol of the Scottish people, but it was depicted in carvings of the royal crown as early as the fourteenth century. From then until the seventeenth century, two unicorns appeared on the royal coat of arms of Scotland. After that time, Scotland and England were joined under one rule, and the royal coat of arms of Great Britain depicted not only a unicorn but also a lion, previously the symbol of England. In this new coat of arms, the lion represented the power of sovereignty and the unicorn symbolized justice and goodness.

Chivalric Knights

Long before the unicorn became associated with Great Britain's coat of arms, the English saw the creature as a symbol of loyalty to country. The reason for this lies in the perception that the unicorn would become violent when provoked. This was the same attitude that the medieval English believed one should take in defense of one's country. Just as the unicorn would fight to the death to avoid capture, so too would an Englishman fight to the death for his country.

Another type of unicorn story emerged and encouraged the English to view the unicorn as symbolic of chivalry, a code of conduct that guided medieval knights. During the Middle Ages it was said that the unicorn's horn had the power to purify drinking water, and that the unicorn used this power to help others rather than itself. As Pool reports,

At sunset, says the legend, the thirsty beasts of the forest gather to drink, but they dare not touch the

The Royal Coat of Arms of Great Britain displays a unicorn, symbolizing justice and goodness.

water lest some wicked serpent, in the heat of the day, has crept up and spat upon it. . . . When the evening shadows are long, the unicorn emerges from the trees. He steps to the shore and plunges his horn in the water, holding it there until all evil is banished. Then he turns and re-enters the forest. Only when his lonely footsteps have died away do the awe-struck creatures rise and drink the pure water.[19]

Under the code of chivalry, knights were charged with placing others' needs above their own, and they viewed themselves as revered protectors of the weak. Therefore, they considered themselves like the unicorn, who had both the power and the self-charged responsibility to help its inferiors. Consequently, Odell Shepard says,

in all the range of animal lore there is no story conceived so completely in the aristocratic spirit [i.e., the spirit of a noble knight] as that of the unicorn stepping down to the poisoned water while the other beasts wait patiently for his coming, and making it safe for them by dipping his magic horn. Here was a perfect emblem of the ideal that European chivalry held before itself in its great periods—the ideal according to which exceptional power and privilege were balanced and justified by exceptional responsibility.[20]

Shepard adds that the unicorn's attraction to fair maidens, its tendency to travel alone, and its ability to move at a swift gallop all made it attractive to medieval knights, who shared these attributes while riding on horseback from town to town. As Shepard explains,

There was something essentially aristocratic [i.e., knightly] about [the unicorn]. His kinship to the

*During the Middle Ages
unicorns came to be asso-
ciated with knights and
the aristocratic spirit.*

horse, always associated with knighthood, was sug-
gestive, but more important was the headlong
enthusiasm of his devotion to beautiful women. He
was fierce and proud and dangerous to his foes, as a
knight should be, and he was also gentle; he had

the dignity of solitude; he was beautiful and strong; most significant of all, he was a protector and champion of other beasts against the wiles of their enemies.[21]

The Personal Unicorn

Whereas knights saw the unicorn as a symbol of a code, a cause, or a country, writers from medieval times to the present have often used the unicorn to symbolize personal longings. To them, the unicorn's purity and goodness, combined with doubts regarding whether the creature was real, were its most important features. In writing about a unicorn these authors were expressing their desire for a purity and goodness that might not truly exist in the world. As scholar Matti Megged says, "For many . . . poets and artists, antique and modern, the Unicorn has existed somehow, somewhere, yet not physically, or it has remained a longing, a dream, a call from another world."[22]

One modern example of this type of symbolism appears in the poem "New Year Letter" by W. H. Auden (1907–1973). Auden uses the unicorn to represent his lost childhood, a time of innocence that—like a unicorn avoiding capture—has escaped him:

> O Unicorn among the cedars,
> To whom no magic charm can lead us.
> White childhood moving like a sigh
> Through the green woods unharmed in thy
> Sophisticated innocence,
> To call thy true love to the dance.[23]

A Romantic Symbol

Many Renaissance authors also used the unicorn to symbolize an individual's acceptance of the unexplainable.

For instance, in the play *The Tempest* by William Shakespeare (1564–1616), when the character of Sebastian sees something wondrous, he exclaims, "Now I will believe/That there are unicorns."[24] Far more common, however, was the use of the unicorn as a symbol of romantic love, a convention that began in the early Middle Ages. As an example, the French poet Thibaut IV (1201–1253), count of Champagne and king of Navarre, once wrote in a love sonnet,

> The unicorn and I are one:
> He also pauses in amaze
> Before some maiden's magic gaze,
> And, while he wonders, is undone.
> On some dear breast he slumbers deep,
> And Treason slays him in that sleep.
> Just so have ended my life's days;
> So Love and my Lady lay me low.
> My heart will not survive this blow.[25]

In his book *The Animal That Never Was*, Matti Megged provides several examples of poets past and present who have compared their love for a woman to the devotion a unicorn has for a maiden in order to say that their love was more pure and faithful than most. Megged says that these poets "found the story of the Unicorn to be the most appropriate symbol of this kind of love."[26]

The romantic unicorn not only appears in a great deal of poetry but also in folktales. In one Scottish folktale, for instance, a unicorn is brought to a palace to stand guard beside a beautiful maiden while she is visited by a series of suitors. Each man who asks to marry the woman shows himself to be crude and violent, and eventually the maiden realizes that she prefers the company of the gentle yet protective unicorn. When she announces that she will marry

the unicorn instead of a human, the unicorn turns into a handsome prince.

The Spiritual Unicorn

A marriage between a woman and a unicorn—or rather, a unicorn man—was featured in the first unicorn story ever to appear in writing. Created in approximately 200 B.C., it was part of a larger work called *The Mahabharata*, which means "The Great Story" in ancient Sanskrit. This unicorn story was based on legends that had been told in India for hundreds of years, and in it the unicorn represents something far greater than romantic love.

The main character is a man named Rsyasrnga, or "Antelope Horn," who has a single horn on his forehead. His mother is a doe, and his father is a human who lives alone in the forest. Rsyasrnga is happy in the forest himself

Often used as a romantic symbol, many Renaissance writers and poets compared their love for a woman to the devotion a unicorn showed a maiden.

until a beautiful girl named Shanta comes to entice him away from his solitary existence.

Shanta is the daughter of a king whose misdeeds have brought drought upon his land. Desperate for rain, he consulted his priests, and they informed him that only Rsyasrnga's presence in the royal court could change the

This modern painting depicts the last episode of the Mahabharata.

weather because his horn had the power to appease the gods. (This is why Shanta was sent to find Rsyasrnga, but she does not tell him this until after he has fallen in love with her and has left the forest.)

When he learns the truth, Rsyasrnga is upset, but he is also filled with sorrow for Shanta's people as he sees the trouble the drought has caused. He begins to cry, and his tears are soon accompanied by rain. Shortly thereafter, Rsyasrnga and Shanta reach her palace, where they are married with her father's blessing.

At the beginning of this story, Rsyasrnga is living the life of an Indian holy man, isolated in the forest. He is also innocent and pure, easily tricked by Shanta. With her encouragement, he disobeys his father's wishes, leaves his life of purity, and travels to the wicked city. There, he learns the truth about Shanta and about the world outside his forest. But rather than allow this knowledge to make him bitter, he is able to set aside his own grief and to grieve for the world instead. Through his tears he purifies and cleanses the landscape, bringing happiness to all.

This story is similar to the story of Jesus Christ, which is the foundation of Christian belief. Christ is sent from heaven by God in order to heal the world; his tears and death bring salvation to sinners. Moreover, anyone who falls to temptation can be restored to God through good works and self-sacrifice. Perhaps this is why Christians long considered the unicorn a symbol of Jesus Christ. Like the creators of the Rsyasrnga legends, they viewed the unicorn in human terms. In fact, scholar Matti Megged suggests that the Rsyasrnga legends influenced later stories emphasizing the human qualities of the unicorn:

> The Indian stories about the Unicorn deal directly with a human creature endowed with the appearance of a Unicorn. But some of the components of these stories are present in later myths of the

Unicorn, where he appears as an animal with one horn, yet behaves in ways similar to those of the Indian human-Unicorn.[27]

Today the unicorn continues to be a religious symbol as well as a symbol of innocence and good fortune. The connections that ancient people made between the unicorn and various human ideals have been strong enough to withstand the passage of time. In fact, the symbolic unicorn has been far more enduring than the concept of a real unicorn. Many people no longer believe that a real unicorn ever existed in the world, but the image of the unicorn remains popular and meaningful.

Chapter 3

Unicorns and Religion

Of all the symbolism associated with the unicorn, the most extensive and complex has been religious in nature. Most of this symbolism is related to Christianity, but some pre-Christian faiths also used the unicorn as a religious symbol. In both cases, the unicorn has been viewed as a representation of human spirituality, not as an animal.

Zoroastrian Scriptures

One of the oldest religions to view the unicorn in spiritual terms was the Zoroastrian religion of ancient Persia (now Iran) in the second century. In this religion two gods, Ormuzd and Ahriman, represent good and evil, respectively, and the god Ormuzd created the unicorn to help him oppose evil. Therefore, the scriptures call for people to "worship the Good Mind and the spirits of the Saints and that sacred beast the Unicorn."[28]

Interestingly, the god Ahriman created the lion to help him oppose goodness. In Zoroastrianism, the lion represented evil because the real beast was dangerous to mankind. As Odell Shepard explains,

The division of the animal kingdom into pure and impure [i.e., good and evil] creatures is made . . .

41

Found at the ancient Persian capital of Persepolis in Iran, this bas-relief sculpture shows processions of unicorns and lions.

according to the utility or hostility of different species to mankind, [and] all the creatures or "servants" of Ormuzd consider it their highest duty to cherish others of their own kind and to destroy the creatures of Ahriman.[29]

The unicorn was viewed as useful to mankind, and therefore good, by virtue of its horn. The ancient Persians believed that the unicorn's horn had the power to purify any water that it touched. This act—the purification of water—was symbolic of the purification of the human soul. In other words, just as a unicorn's horn could cleanse polluted water, so too could the worship of the unicorn cleanse a corrupt spirit. Therefore, the Zoroastrian scriptures say of the unicorn,

With that horn it will vanquish and dissipate all the vile corruption due to the efforts of noxious [harmful] creatures. . . . If, O [unicorn]! you were not created for the water, all the water in the sea would have perished from the contamination which the poison of the Evil Spirit brought into its water through the death of the creatures of Ahuramazd [Ormuzd].[30]

No one knows when the unicorn first became associated with water purification or why. Shepard suggests that the unicorn's connection to water might have been inspired by its appearance. Since the ancient Persians thought that the unicorn was white, perhaps its image reminded them of a cloud. Its horn, Shepard says, might therefore have been seen as a lightning bolt. If this was indeed how ancient people viewed the unicorn, then it might explain why in many early religions the unicorn was believed to dwell in the heavens as a servant of the gods.

Perfect and Solitary

Regardless of how it came about, the unicorn's connection to purification appears in many religions throughout the world. Buddhists, for example, associate the unicorn with spiritual improvement and use its horn to symbolize Nirvana, the highest of all spiritual states. A person who has reached Nirvana has transcended all bodily desires and, in ultimate peace, has a soul ready to be absorbed by God. The unicorn embodies this perfection and contentment by virtue of its goodness and peaceful nature.

Moreover, because the unicorn is a solitary animal, Buddhists see solitude as a way for humans to achieve this perfection and contentment. Consequently, one Buddhist hymn recommends that people adopt the unicorn's habits:

The deer untethered roams the wild
Where it wishes in search of food
Seeing this liberty, wise man,

Fare solit'ry [solitary] as the Unicorn.
Free everywhere and at odds with none
Content with what comes your way
Enduring peril without alarm,
Fare solit'ry as the Unicorn
Like a lion fearless of the howling pack
Like the breeze ne'er trapped in a snare
Like the lotus unsoiled by its stagnant pool,
Fare solit'ry as the Unicorn.[31]

Buddhists believe that the unicorn followed the Buddha and protects his birthplace.

To Buddhists, the unicorn's quiet, solitary spirit is an ideal to which the human spirit should aspire. But the Buddhists also value the unicorn's legendary ability to protect and defend. Buddhists believe that a unicorn came to the founder of their religion, Siddhartha Gautama, known as the Buddha, when he gave his first sermon in Benares, India, sometime during the sixth century B.C. After listening to the Buddha speak, the unicorn knelt at his feet as a sign of loyalty and devotion. From that time on, according to Buddhist stories, the unicorn has protected the place where the Buddha was born.

In one such story, a thireenth-century Mongol

warrior named Genghis Khan was ready to invade and pillage the Buddha's birthplace when he was confronted by a unicorn that kneeled three times at his feet. Deciding that this was a warning from God not to proceed, Genghis Khan left the region immediately. For this reason, Buddhists associate the unicorn with salvation as well as perfection.

A Symbol for Christ

Christians, too, have traditionally seen the unicorn as a symbol of both salvation and perfection. But unlike Buddhists, they have viewed the unicorn as representative of a supreme being. During the Middle Ages, Christians decided that the unicorn was a symbol for Jesus Christ, whom their religion teaches was the son of God born of the Virgin Mary.

This Spanish painting shows the Virgin Mary holding a unicorn. Christians during the Middle Ages associated the unicorn with Christ.

One reason that this association occurred has to do with similarities between the story of Christ's life and the many unicorn stories told during the Middle Ages. To medieval people—as with ancient Persians—the unicorn was a spiritually pure being with a gentle nature and the ability to cleanse water with the touch of its horn. Christ was also spiritually pure and gentle and, according to the Bible, used water to cleanse human souls.

Early Christians first noted these similarities in a collection of animal stories called the *Physiologus*, which appeared in approximately A.D. 200. No one knows who wrote these stories, or even whether they were first written in Greek or in Hebrew. Nonetheless, they spread quickly throughout Europe and the Middle East; there are medieval translations of the *Physiologus* in such diverse languages as Arabic, Latin, Armenian, Old High German, Icelandic, Old French, Ethiopic, Italian, and Anglo-Saxon. One of the earliest versions of the *Physiologus* said that Christ was like the unicorn because he "raised up for us a horn of salvation."[32] This refers to the purification powers of the horn and of Christ.

During the fourteenth and fifteenth centuries, new versions of the *Physiologus* appeared that called Christ "the spiritual Unicorn," and said that the unicorn's horn "signifies the words of the savior [Christ]: 'I and my Father are one' (John 10:30)."[33] At that time, the unicorn's horn was believed to be shaped as though two straight horns had been twisted to make one. Therefore, people decided that the unicorn's horn symbolized not only the power to heal souls but also the union between God and Christ in heaven—the ultimate source of healing power.

There were many other elements of the *Physiologus* unicorn story that took on religious significance. Although there are several variations of this story, the essential details are the same: The unicorn encounters a maiden in the forest, lays his head in her lap, and becomes docile enough to be captured by hunters, whereupon he is taken to a king's palace. The maiden was believed to represent Mary, Christ's mother. Mary and Christ had a close relationship, as did the unicorn and the maiden, and like Mary, the maiden was always a virgin. Moreover, Mary was with Jesus around the time of his death but could do nothing to protect him from his assailants. Similarly, the maiden in unicorn stories can only watch as hunters capture the unicorn. In most versions of the story she is an unwilling participant in this drama—either unwittingly helping the hunters or forced to do so   and although her presence makes the unicorn docile, she does not restrain him in any way.

Even more significant was the similarity between the attitudes that Christ and the unicorn display while being captured. In the unicorn story, hunters do not have any trouble leading the unicorn away; the creature is meek and surrenders without a fight. The same was true for Christ, who went with his executioners without a struggle. Perhaps more importantly, the meekness of both the unicorn and Christ was not due to a lack of power; both beings could easily have overcome those who hunted them, yet both accepted their destiny with compliance. And because the

Medieval and Renaissance artwork depicting unicorns and maidens were usually meant to represent the relationship between Christ and the Virgin Mary.

unicorn was thought to be a creature of self-sacrifice—helping others rather than itself, just as Christ did—medieval people believed that the unicorn accepted death for the same reason Christ did: By dying, it purified humanity and cleansed people of their sins.

Many medieval and Renaissance writers expressed this sentiment in stories and poems. For instance, a German folk song of the period, as recorded in the nineteenth century in Ludwig Uhland's work "Alte hoch-und-neiderdeutsche Volkslieder" ("Old High- and Low-German Folksongs"), says in part,

> What would be now the state of us,
> But for this Unicorn,
> And what be the fate of us,
> Poor sinners, lost, forlorn?
> Oh, may He leap us on and up,
> Unworthy though we be,
> Into his Father's kingdom
> To dwell eternally.[34]

Through the same reasoning, medieval people believed that the part of the unicorn story in which the unicorn is taken to the king's palace represents Christ's journey to heaven after his death, particularly since Christians often refer to heaven as God's kingdom. As one fourteenth-century German scholar, Konad von Megenberg (1309-1374), wrote, "Christ, like the Unicorn, was captured by the wicked hunters and by them shamefully put to death. [But] the Unicorn rose again and went heavenward, to the Palace of the heavenly King."[35]

Religious Imagery

Medieval people typically viewed the hunters who took the unicorn to the king's palace in one of two ways. Some thought that the hunters represented the people who put Christ to death; meanwhile, others thought that the hunters represented the angels who took Christ to heaven after his death. These differing interpretations of unicorn hunt scenes appeared in many medieval and Renaissance works of art. In several of these, the hunters were clearly depicted as angels; one of the earliest unicorn hunt paintings, a fifteenth-century German fresco, shows the archangel Gabriel—a common religious image during this period—hunting the unicorn. Gabriel also appears as a unicorn hunter in several other pieces of art, including an early sixteenth-century German tapestry currently on display in the Bavarian National Museum in Munich, Germany.

Because the archangel Gabriel was a familiar figure to Renaissance people, the religious nature of such artwork was unmistakable. Everyone who saw the unicorn in a painting with Gabriel knew that the animal was supposed to represent Christ. The same is true for the many Renaissance paintings that show the unicorn with a maiden who is clearly the Virgin Mary. Artists of the period generally painted Mary in the same way, with a halo above her head, making her image easily recognizable.

Some scenes in unicorn artwork were also easily recognized as religious imagery. For example, in several medieval paintings the unicorn is being stabbed in the side with a spear, much as Christ was stabbed in the side with a spear while on the cross. Moreover, the wound on the unicorn is bleeding in a way typical of Christ's wound in traditional religious artwork. In some scenes of the hunt, the hunters are accompanied by four dogs labeled "Truth," "Righteousness," "Placidity," and "Compassion." Medieval Christians were well aware that these traits were sacred Christian virtues.

The Cloisters Tapestries

Not all medieval unicorn artwork, however, had obvious religious imagery. For example, a famous series of unicorn tapestries on display at the Cloisters, a part of the Metropolitan Museum of Art in New York City, depicts a

The Cloisters tapestries depict a unicorn hunt that does not appear to have any religious connotations.

unicorn hunt that does not appear to have a connection to Christ. There are seven tapestries in the series, which was most likely created in approximately 1500 in Brussels, Belgium. The first tapestry shows a group of noblemen preparing for a hunt; the second, a unicorn drinking from a fountain as the concealed hunters prepare to attack it. In the third tapestry the unicorn is fleeing from its attackers, but in the fourth it is engaged in battle with them. In the fifth tapestry it is being subdued by a maiden as a hunter watches from the bushes. The sixth tapestry shows one unicorn being stabbed while another is being carried to a castle. In the seventh and final tapestry, the unicorn is once again alive, but it is no longer free. Instead, it is corralled beneath a tree in a beautiful garden.

To a modern viewer, there appears to be no religious imagery in these tapestries. In fact, some scholars believe that the tapestries' unicorn hunt symbolizes a bachelor's conquest by a maiden, with the enclosed garden representing marriage. Matti Megged suggests that the tapestries are nothing more than a hunting story, with no religious significance behind the scenes: "These tapestries represent a fantastic, beautiful, probably mysterious animal that somehow invaded 'realistic' scenes of a hunt, referring

Some scholars believe that the seventh Cloisters tapestry represents a bachelor being trapped by marriage.

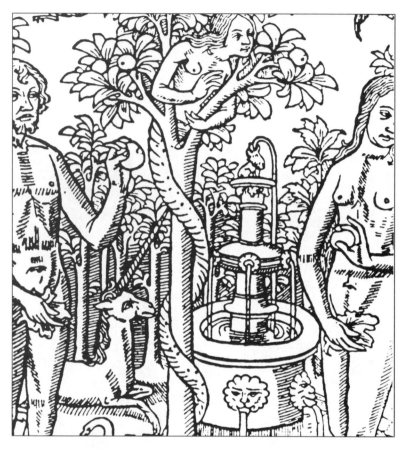

Many Renaissance artists showed the unicorn with Adam and Eve in the Garden of Eden.

more to a typical historical background of hunting than to a sacred one."[36]

Nonetheless, a sixteenth-century viewer would most likely have interpreted these tapestries as religious art because the unicorn was so deeply connected to Christianity by then that most people assumed any artist depicting a unicorn intended to symbolize Christ. For the same reason, they probably would have believed that the enclosed garden represented heaven.

Biblical Associations

Moreover, by the time the tapestries were made, the unicorn had long been associated with the Garden of Eden. Many Renaissance paintings, drawings, and mosaics showed the unicorn with Adam and Eve in the garden, and, according to a popular story, the unicorn was the first animal named by Adam in Eden. Some early Hebrews believed that this honor—being named first—made the unicorn sacred.

But the Garden of Eden was not the only biblical image to be employed in unicorn art and literature. Another popular scene from the Bible to be associated with the unicorn was that of Noah loading the ark. According to the Old Testament of the Bible, Noah placed a male and female of every animal species on board his ark so they would survive a great flood sent by God. During the Middle Ages, storytellers suggested that the reason no one ever saw a unicorn—although they were mentioned in the Old Testament of the Bible—was that the unicorns arrived too late to board the ark. In a variation of this story, the unicorns made Noah angry and he refused to allow them on his ark.

There are seven references to the unicorn in the Old Testament, but they are fairly casual mentions of an apparently real animal. For example, in one passage in the King James version of the Bible, God is said to have "the strength of the unicorn" (Num. 23:20). Another passage says, "But my horn shalt thou exalt like the horn of the unicorn: I shall be anointed with fresh oil" (Ps. 92:10).

Despite these references, the Bible does not tell of a unicorn being named by Adam or trying to board the ark. Nonetheless, many medieval people believed these stories on faith because they thought that if the Bible mentioned an animal it had to have existed. The Noah story was simply one way to explain why unicorns were not a living part of the medieval world.

The Unicorn's Promise

One element of the religious symbolism associated with the unicorn/Noah story still exists today; modern unicorn artwork often includes a rainbow somewhere in the picture. The rainbow is a symbol of the Great Flood because, in the biblical Noah story, the rainbow was a sign of God's promise not to produce another such flood. Some modern Christians believe that the unicorn is the same type of symbol because it represents Christ, and Christ offers the promise of salvation to his followers. In other words, both the rainbow and unicorn are symbols of God's love for mankind.

A modern Christian, Roy Wilkinson, expresses this sentiment in his book *Are You a Unicorn? The Mission and Meaning of Unicorns* when he says,

> Why is the unicorn often pictured with a rainbow in the background? The answer is that the rainbow is also a symbol of a promise that God has made to mankind. Shortly after the great Flood in which God destroys the wicked people of the earth, God blesses Noah and his son. . . . Then God makes a covenant [agreement] with Noah and his sons and all living creatures upon the face of the earth that "neither shall there any more be a flood to destroy the earth." Then God . . . [offers the rainbow] as a symbol to remind us of the promise that God has made to us concerning the flood. The unicorn is a symbol to remind us of the promise that God has made to bless all of the families of the earth. The two symbols of God's promises to man go well together.[37]

Wilkinson and some other modern Christians continue to consider the unicorn an important religious symbol representing essential characteristics of Christianity. Wilkinson calls Christ "the model unicorn" and says that like Christ, the modern unicorn stands for "fighting for truth, justice, goodness, and purity, and helping the downtrodden, the underdogs, the sick, and the weary."[38] To Wilkinson, anyone who lives a good life, but particularly a person who acts as a healing force in the world, is a human manifestation of the unicorn.

Since the mid–sixteenth century, most Christians have seen it as improper to depict unicorns in religous artwork.

But although some modern Christians see the unicorn as a Christian symbol, the official position of many Christian churches is that the unicorn is a secular symbol, suitable only for adorning such items as children's bedroom furniture or stationery. In 1563 the Roman Catholic Church decreed that depicting Jesus Christ in artwork as a unicorn or any other unusual symbol ran contrary to church teachings. From that point on, the Catholic Church no longer paid artists to create unicorn art, nor did the church promote it. Without church sanction, the use of the symbol as a religious image greatly diminished, and today the unicorn is seen far more often in secular art than in religious art.

Chapter 4

Magic and Medicine

To some people, the unicorn has had value as a symbol or mythological being. But to others, it has had monetary and medicinal value instead. From ancient times through the Renaissance, products appeared in marketplaces that were said to be made from a unicorn's horn—drinking cups, carvings, and powder, for example. These items were in high demand because people believed that a unicorn's horn had the power to cure illness, protect against poisoning, and bring good luck to the owner of the horn.

Magical Horns

Many ancient and primitive people believed that horns of any kind were magical or lucky. In fact, Odell Shepard reports that there was an "almost world-wide use of horns as charms and amulets"[39] among primitive peoples to bring good luck. According to Shepard, the idea that horns were lucky often led to the belief that horns could cure sickness. He says that in some instances,

> all horns came to be regarded as medicinal because they were vaguely associated with beneficent supernatural powers, although in reality there was no relationship of cause and effect but merely an overlapping. Such overlapping is unmistakable when one looks, for example, at the pharmacopoeia [medicines]

of a Zulu medicine man, which consists usually of nothing but fifteen or twenty short antelope horns tied together by thongs.[40]

In other words, primitive people—such as the Zulus in Africa—often used horns as medicine, even though there was no proof that horns actually worked as medicine.

Beliefs about the positive effects of horns in general were applied to the unicorn horn in particular after the ancient Greek physician Ctesias wrote about the unicorn's medicinal power. He was the first person to suggest in writing that a unicorn's horn could cure someone of an illness and protect against poisoning:

Many African tribes believed that the horns of animals could be used as medicine.

The dust filed from [the unicorn's] horn is administered in a potion as a protection against deadly drugs. . . . Those who drink out of these horns, made into drinking vessels, are not subject, they say, to convulsions or to the holy disease [epilepsy]. Indeed, they are immune even to poisons if, either before or after swallowing such, they drink wine, water, or anything else from these beakers.[41]

Stories Spread

At a time when horns were considered powerful charms and unicorns were believed to be real beasts, Ctesias's words were quickly accepted as fact, and Greek traders soon passed this information on to people in the Middle East. These people in turn carried the story into Europe. Elizabeth Pool explains:

Baghdad, on the banks of the Tigris [a river in Arabia], was the hub of radiating caravan routes where, through the centuries, Greece and Egypt, Persia and India, exchanged facts and fancies. Under the Arabs, "Baghdad the Glorious" became a center for every branch of art and learning and a hotbed for every folly. Wave after wave of Arab philosophers and poets, mathematicians and architects, went forth from Baghdad and entered Europe. . . . With them went physicians carrying in their heads and on their scrolls a rich concoction of wisdom and fantasy—including the ideas of Ctesias.[42]

Ctesias's comments spread throughout the Roman Empire with the help of Roman scholars like Aelianus, who repeated the Greek's ideas in his own works. According to Aelianus, "It is said that whosoever drinks from [the unicorn's] horn is safe from all incurable diseases such as convulsions and the so-called holy disease, and that he cannot be killed by poison."[43]

Because respected scholars like Aelianus mentioned the power of the unicorn's horn, people began to seek it as medicine and as an antidote to poison. Beginning in the early thirteenth century, sailors brought strange-looking horns from distant shores—horns that looked nothing like any horn Europeans had ever seen before—and said they were from unicorns.

These horns were six to eight feet in length, thick at the base and narrow at the tip, and had an odd spiraled appearance, as though two horns had been twisted around each other into one. Moreover, despite this twisting, each horn made a straight line from base to tip, which meant that they could not be mistaken for the rhinoceros horns and elephant tusks common in the European marketplace; all other types of horns and tusks familiar to Europeans at that time were curved.

An Oddity on Display

When the first of these so-called unicorn horns—which soon became known by the shorter term *alicorn*—appeared in Europe, they were considered such an oddity that they were put on display and tourists flocked to view them. One such alicorn was the famed horn of St. Denis (a church near Paris, France); it was approximately seven feet long and weighed more than 13 pounds. One traveler who saw the horn, Girolamo Cardan, later wrote,

> After we had seen the sepulchres of the kings and the statues and other marble ornaments, I studied very closely the unicorn's horn hanging in the sanctuary. It was so long that I could not touch the top of it with my hand, but its thickness was slight in proportion to its length, for it was easily possible to surround it with the thumb and first finger. . . . It

Constructed in 1665 for King Frederick III of Denmark, the pillars on this throne were once said to be made of unicorn horns.

was smooth all over, but was marked by bands run-ning from end to end as on a snail-shell. . . . Nature makes nothing else that I know of like this.[44]

The horn of St. Denis was plain and was displayed with one end resting in water. Other alicorns were decorated with gold, silver, and/or jewels. Many sat on ornate gold or silver stands, some of which looked like candlesticks. Most alicorns were whole, but some were broken. This was the case with an alicorn at St. Mark's Cathedral in Venice,

Italy, which was in three pieces. Brought to Italy from lands unknown, it had sacred writing on it in Greek and Arabic.

Some of the most decorated alicorns had been bejeweled in order to hide unsightly scraping marks, where people had scored them to get alicorn powder. In fact, one Italian governing body, the Council of Ten, decreed during the Renaissance that all churches "are to have the Alicorns decorated with silver from the points to the silver-gilt handles so that the marks of former scrapings may be concealed, and they are to prohibit any further scrapings except in cases allowed by unanimous vote of the Council of Ten."[45]

Alicorn Prescriptions

Shortly after the first alicorns reached European marketplaces, physicians began prescribing powder made from the horns to cure a variety of ills. When patients recovered, physicians assumed that the alicorn was responsible. For example, after the daughter of King Henry II of France was successfully treated in 1557 with alicorn powder—which had been dissolved in water as a smallpox cure—people credited the alicorn for her survival. Had she died, they would simply have assumed that she had not been given the cure soon enough, so strong was their belief in the alicorn's power.

As word of such cures spread, medical texts began to list alicorn—usually in powdered form—as standard treatment for many illnesses. For example the seventeenth-century medical text *Pharmacopoeia Medico-Chymica,* by Johann Schröder, recommended specific doses of powdered alicorn for various infectious diseases as well as for epilepsy in infants. In other texts, alicorn was said to cure plague, rabies, worms, and memory loss as well. Rumor also said that ingesting alicorn powder could prolong youth, and that if some of this substance were placed on a dead person's tongue that person would come back to life.

Alicorn powder was commonly purchased in apothecary shops, and from 1651 until 1741, every registered pharmacist in London was required by the English Royal Society of Physicians to have alicorn in some form on hand. In addition to powder, this included pieces of alicorn, which were said to protect general health when worn as amulets. Also available was a product called *eau de licorne*, which was simply water in which an alicorn had been soaked. Sold by the quart or pint, it was prescribed by physicians for such illnesses as gout, scurvy, convulsions, bowel obstructions, and depression.

Some apothecaries also offered substances they said came from other parts of the unicorn. Powdered unicorn liver was particularly popular because of the writings of the twelfth-century German abbess Hildegarde of Bingen. A respected authority on medical treatment, she said that

Two unicorns decorate the doorway of an apothecary in London. For hundreds of years, apothecaries sold alicorn as a cure for various illnesses.

ingesting a concoction of egg yolk and powdered unicorn's liver would cure leprosy; likewise, she claimed that wearing a belt and boots made of unicorn skin would protect against fevers and bubonic plague, respectively. She also said that there was a hard object at the base of a genuine alicorn. Some said it was crystallized blood or a ruby, although Hildegarde insisted it was clear rather than red and therefore of unknown matter. It was rumored that this object was perhaps more powerful than the alicorn itself and that it could protect people from evil thoughts and nightmares. Thus, some apothecaries offered what they claimed was this object for sale as well.

Protection Against Poisoning

Alicorns reached the height of their popularity during the Middle Ages when they were believed to be a protection against poisoning. Poison was a common weapon in medieval society, and there were many instances of people advancing themselves politically and economically by murdering a foe with poison. Odell Shepard says that,

> according to general belief, a clever poisoner could compound a drug that would kill in an hour, a week, or a month, as pleasure and convenience might dictate. . . . So sensible and well-trained a man as Ambroise Paré, trusted physician to the court of France . . . thought that it was possible to kill a man by placing poison under the saddle on which he habitually rode. Pope Clement VII, who owned several alicorns and gave away as many more, was thought to have been killed by the odours of a poisoned torch. Poison might be hidden in flowers, in gloves, in rings and bracelets, in cosmetics. How could it be escaped? . . . There was no real security unless one could find a means of detecting poison the instant it was brought near

one, and upon this task, therefore, . . . great sums of money were for a long time expended.[46]

In an attempt to protect themselves from poisoning, every nobleman wanted a whole alicorn horn that could be carved into goblets, cups, bowls, or spoons. In fact, during the seventeenth and early eighteenth centuries all French kings used spoons with alicorn handles. Kings everywhere also had servants dip a piece of alicorn into their wine before they drank it to ensure the liquid was not poisonous. Many authors of the period extolled the benefits of using alicorn to protect oneself against poisoning. For example, in his book *Historie of Foure-Footed Beasts,* English clergyman Edward Topsell (1572–1625) writes,

> The horns of Unicorns, . . . being beaten and drunk in water, doth wonderfully help against poison: as of late experience doth manifest unto us, a man, who having taken poison and beginning to swell was preserved by this remedy. I myself have heard of a man worthy to be believed, that having eaten a poisoned cherry, and perceiving his belly to swell, he cured himself by the marrow of this horn being drunk in Wine.[47]

Topsell also provided tips on how to make alicorn powder more palatable as a poison remedy, suggesting that the horn be "beaten and boiled in Wine" or mixed with "Amber, Ivory dust, leaves of gold, coral, & certain other things . . . and beaten in the decoction of Raisins and Cinnamon" before being "cast . . . in water." He added that such efforts would not be necessary if, like "the ancient writers," people everywhere were able to obtain "cups made of this horn."[48]

The sixteenth-century zoologist Conrad Geisner—a highly respected scientist of his day—also advocated ingesting alicorn to ward off poison. In addition, some of his

peers advocated placing an alicorn on a dining table as a centerpiece, believing that an alicorn would actually "sweat" if poison were nearby. No one knows how this belief began, but John Swan, in his 1635 work *Speculum Mundi*, reflected the common belief: "This horne hath many sovereign virtues, insomuch that being put upon a table furnished with many junkets and banqueting dishes, it will quickly descrie [reveal] whether there be any poyson [poison] or venime [venom] among them, for if there be the horne is presently covered with a kind of sweat or dew."[49]

This unicorn drawing is taken from the front page of Grundtlicher underricht, *a 1546 book on medicine. Doctors believed that unicorns' horns would cure diseases and ward off poisons.*

Testing for Fraud

Because medieval people perceived alicorns as being effective against poisoning, noblemen were willing to pay extremely high prices for them. For instance, in the mid-1500s the Holy Roman Emperor Charles V gave a nobleman two alicorns worth approximately 1 million of today's dollars in order to settle a debt. In 1558 the royal treasury of England contained an alicorn worth 10,000 pounds, the price of a large estate. Even a small piece of alicorn might be worth as much as ten times its weight in gold.

But sometimes a nobleman did not get the protection for which he had paid so much. For example, King James I of England paid ten thousand pounds sterling for an alicorn he believed to be genuine, but when he asked for a demonstration of its powers he was disappointed; a servant who drank a mixture of its powder and some poison quickly died.

King James's test of his alicorn's effectiveness against poison was a certain one, but not many people were willing to accept the risk associated with such a test. Consequently, other means of testing a horn's powers were devised, including feeding two pigeons poison and then give only one of them scrapings from an alicorn as an antidote. If the poison was strong enough to kill the pigeon that did not receive the alicorn but did not harm the other pigeon, then the alicorn being tested was genuine. Few people ever considered that the affected pigeon might have died for other reasons or that the surviving pigeon might have done better than its companion because it was healthier and could resist that particular dose of poison.

Another popular test was to drop a whole alicorn or a piece of alicorn into water to see if bubbles formed around it as it fell. It was said that only genuine alicorns bubbled, and few people considered that the way the alicorn was dropped might affect the way the water responded.

One person who doubted the bubble test was a Hebrew physician named David de Pomis. De Pomis criticized it in his 1587 book *Dittionario Novo Hebraico*. However, the test he devised to replace the bubble test was no more scientific:

> The common test which consists in placing the object in water to see whether bubbles will rise is not at all to be trusted, and therefore, wishing to benefit the world and to expose the wicked persons who sell worthless things at great prices, I take this occasion to describe a true test by which one may know the genuine horn from the false. The test is this: place the horn in a vessel of any sort of material you like, and with it three or four live and large scorpions, keeping the vessel covered. If you find four hours later that the scorpions are dead, or almost lifeless, the alicorn is a good one, and there is not money enough in the world to pay for it. Otherwise, it is false.[50]

Alicorn was considered so valuable that King James I of England once paid £10000 for an alicorn.

De Pomis did not consider that the scorpions in his test—chosen because they had poisonous venom and alicorns were reputed to neutralize poisonous things—might have died for reasons other than the alicorn's presence. The creatures could have died of shock, starvation, or maltreatment; nonetheless most people believed that the alicorn's power was responsible for their demise.

Many people believed that the horns of unicorns, like the one shown in this 1840 woodcut, would counteract venom from scorpions, spiders, and other poisonous creatures.

This was true for other insect-related tests as well. A particularly popular one involved poisonous spiders, which were placed either within a circle drawn on the floor using the tip of an alicorn or in water into which an alicorn had been soaked. If the alicorn were genuine, it was believed that the spiders would not leave the circle and would eventually die of starvation there. But again, most people did not consider that the spiders might have remained within the circle and died there for reasons other than the alicorn.

Doubts Surface

A few individuals, however, did doubt the alicorn's effectiveness against poisoning. For instance, sixteenth-century physician Ambroise Paré (1510–1590) reported that he had never found alicorn to be useful against poisons. In his book *Of Poysons*, he writes,

> Grant there be Unicornes, must it therefore follow that their hornes must be of such efficacy against

poysons? If we judge by events, and the experience of things, I can protest thus much, that I have often made tryall thereof, yet could I never find any good successe in the use thereof against poisons, in such as I have had in cure.[51]

Moreover, Paré insisted that reputable physicians had stopped prescribing alicorn for poisoning, and that even for other illnesses there was no proof that alicorn worked any better than ivory—a substance that came from walrus and elephant tusks. Consequently, he says, "I prescribe Ivory to such as are poor, and Unicornes horn to the rich, as that they so much desire."[52]

But although physicians of the sixteenth and seventeenth centuries increasingly spoke out against the use of alicorn as a cure-all, alicorns continued to hold their value until the eighteenth century. The people who sold alicorn—who were more concerned with profit than with public health—insisted that alicorns had great medicinal value, and many patients so believed in the power of the alicorn that they demanded their doctors prescribe it.

However, lower classes held on to their faith in the alicorn far longer than the noblemen who paid high prices for whole alicorns. During the seventeenth century, as explorers and scientists expanded humankind's knowledge about the world, most educated people learned that there were other animals besides unicorns that could be the source of the horns. Moreover, many so-called alicorns were complete frauds.

One of the most common ways to make a fraudulent alicorn was to boil an elephant or walrus tusk for six hours in a special solution that softened it, at which point its curved shape could be straightened out. The surface of the tusk was then scored to simulate the twisting of an alicorn. Far less effort was required to counterfeit alicorn powder and pieces. Whereas alicorn pieces were usually chips of elephant or walrus tusk, alicorn powder was often made from ground bones, fossilized animals, clay, or limestone.

As noblemen realized that alicorns were most likely not from unicorns and that their medicinal value was questionable, prices for alicorns fell. Between 1612 and 1669 in Frankfurt, Germany, for example, the price of alicorn pieces dropped from 128 florins (gold coins) per ounce to 8. Between 1630 and 1649 in London, the value of a large whole alicorn in excellent condition dropped from 8,000 pounds to 600.

By the eighteenth century alicorns were no longer in demand among the upper classes. As Odell Shepard reports,

Many "genuine" alicorns were made from boiled elephant tusks that had been straightened out and made to look like alicorns.

By 1734 a well-informed writer could say that horns which formerly brought many thousands of dollars could then be had for twenty-five; yet this same writer makes it clear that even in his time there was still an active sale, and it is certain that long after the wealthy had lost all interest in alicorns the poor continued to buy them.[53]

By the end of the eighteenth century, however, even the lower classes had decided that alicorns had little value, either medicinal or economic. The public no longer demanded that physicians prescribe alicorn, and by the nineteenth century it was no longer listed as a cure in most medical texts. From that point on, alicorns were bought and sold—at a fraction of their former price—primarily as decorative items.

Chapter 5

Searching for a Real Unicorn

By the nineteenth century, many people had decided that alicorns were not really unicorn horns. Yet most people found it hard to believe that unicorns were entirely fictional given all of the stories and scholarly writings about them. As Charles Gould wrote in 1886 in his book *Mythical Monsters*, "I find it impossible to believe that a creature whose existence has been affirmed by so many authors, at so many different dates, and from so many different countries, can be, as mythologists demand, merely the symbol of a myth."[54]

A New Discovery

In ancient times, people accepted unicorn reports without needing proof of their accuracy. No one demanded that Ctesias, for instance, produce a live unicorn to prove that his comments about them were correct. Back then, much about the world was learned through hearsay and accepted on faith. Belief did not depend on eyewitness experiences.

During the Renaissance this attitude began to change; the rise of science encouraged people to question the accuracy of theories and to seek out evidence to support them. But by this time alicorns were already on the market, and they seemed proof enough that unicorns were real.

Then, in 1577, an explorer named Martin Frobisher made a discovery that would eventually affect the way people viewed the alicorn. While trying to find a northwest passage from England to the Far East, he and his fellow sailors saw something unusual floating in the water. It looked like a fish, but coming out of its face was what appeared to Frobisher to be a unicorn's horn. He and his crew took the creature from the water and tested the horn, which was broken at the tip, by putting spiders inside of it. When the spiders died, the men believed they had discovered a sea unicorn, or *licornes de mer*.

What they had really found, however, was a narwhal, an arctic sea mammal somewhat similar to a dolphin. Males of the species have a seven- to nine-foot-long pure ivory tusk—not a horn—growing from the left side of the upper jaw as an elongation of a tooth. Because narwhals do

Most Europeans believed that the existence of the narwhal, or "sea unicorn," proved that unicorns were real.

not travel outside of the arctic and because they cannot survive in captivity, Frobisher and his European companions had never seen such an animal before. With all of the unicorn stories circulating in Europe at that time, it makes sense that the seamen associated the narwhal with a unicorn.

Had Frobisher made his discovery in modern times, most people would have immediately suspected that the narwhal was the source of alicorns. After all, the main suppliers of alicorns to the European market were sailors and Scandinavian fishermen. But when Frobisher shared his discovery with his peers, most did not become suspicious. Instead, they believed that the existence of the narwhal proved unicorns were real. The reason for this lies in the fact that medieval people were certain that every animal on land had a counterpart in the sea. Therefore, if there was a sea unicorn—a narwhal—then there had to be a land unicorn as well.

The Truth Revealed

Still, as time passed a few people began to have doubts about their alicorns. For example, sixteenth-century zoologist Pierre Belon wrote that the alicorn was surely some kind of walrus tusk, and scholar Andrea Marini suggested that alicorns had to come from the sea. Another scholar, Goropius of Antwerp, wrote in 1569, "I sometimes suspect that this is the horn of some fish, because many remarkable horns are found among fishes and also because this horn at Antwerp was brought from Iceland."[55]

Then, in 1638, an investigation marked the beginning of the end of people's faith in the alicorn as proof that unicorns were real. At that time, Danish zoologist and professor Ole Wurm undertook a careful study prompted by merchants curious about the origin of their alicorns. Wurm traced the origin of alicorns and learned that Scandinavian fishermen had indeed been supplying Europe with narwhal, rather than unicorn, horns. Traders had kept the origin of their wares a secret because only unicorn horns would have commanded a high price. In addition, Scandinavian kings restricted the number of alicorns sent to Europe not only because scarcity kept prices high but also because the unicorn was supposed to be a rare animal.

Wurm shared this information in a dissertation, along with his conclusion that alicorns were not horns but teeth. To Europeans, the news that alicorns were teeth and not horns was even worse than the news that they came from narwhals rather than unicorns. Horns had long been considered lucky; teeth were not. An adviser to the grand duke of Moscow, reflected the prevailing sentiment when, in 1647, he advised the duke not to buy a large alicorn from the Company of New Greenland Merchants, the biggest purveyor of alicorns, because it was just "the tooth of a fish."[56]

Searching for a Live Unicorn

Once alicorns were no longer accepted as definitive proof that unicorns were real, people began to seek other evi-

Many theories circulated as to the unicorn's native habitat.

dence of unicorns. The most obvious evidence, of course, was a living beast; therefore, many people set out in search of the unicorn's native habitat. Various locations were proposed for each search. One theory was that unicorns lived on some undiscovered arctic island because the region was so hospitable to the narwhal and so far from human contact. Another location often suggested as the unicorn's habitat was some remote region of Asia, a place long associated with the mythological unicorn. This region was also considered the likely habitat because several prominent explorers

It was rumored that the Christian emperor Prester John possessed several unicorns in his court.

had claimed to have seen the unicorn in Asia. For instance, Vincent Le Blanc wrote in 1567 that he had observed unicorns in royal courts throughout the Orient, adding, "There are some persons who doubt whether this animal is to be found anywhere in the world I am well aware, but in addition to my own observation there are several serious writers who bear witness to its existence."[57]

Prester John

Another prominent explorer who reported seeing unicorns in Asia was Edward Webbe, an Englishman who toured the region during the reign of Queen Elizabeth. Specifically, he said that he had observed several unicorns in India in the court of a Christian emperor named Prester John. Webbe later wrote, "I have seene in a place like a Park adjoyning unto prester Iohn's [John's] Court, three score and seven-teene unicornes and eliphants all alive at one time, and they were so tame that I have played with them as one would play with young Lambes."[58]

Stories about the court of Prester John had been circulating in Europe since the twelfth century. It was said that this court had all manner of wondrous beasts, including the unicorn. From the outset, these stories were accepted as fact rather than fantasy. The reason for this has to do with the way in which the stories began. In the twelfth century, a letter surfaced in Europe that was supposedly written by Prester John himself describing his lands. Because it was a letter, people never thought that it might be fiction; letters were not commonly the way storytellers presented fictional tales at that time.

However, during this period literature was passed on through transcription, with each new copy being rewritten by hand. Transcribers were not always careful about maintaining the original version of a work, and in the case of the Prester John letter, various changes were made with each copy. Even more changes occurred as the letter was translated into different languages. Over time, Prester John's kingdom was relocated from Asia to Africa, and its creatures became more and more exotic. However, the unicorn appears in every version.

In many versions of the Prester John letter, the unicorn was mentioned in connection with the lion. For example, one version reads,

> There are in our land also unicorns who have in front a single horn of which there are three kinds: green, black, and white. Sometimes they kill lions. But a lion kills them in a very subtle way. When a unicorn is tired it lies down by a tree. The lion goes then behind it and when the unicorn wants to strike him with his horn, it dashes into the tree with such a force that it cannot free itself. Then the lion kills it.[59]

Although pairing the unicorn with the lion was common in unicorn mythology, most medieval people still did not suspect that the Prester John stories might be fiction rather than fact.

Today most scholars think otherwise; they theorize that the original Prester John letter was a work of fiction, perhaps written by a Western monk who wanted to encourage the belief that a powerful Christian emperor existed in non-Christian Asia. But in medieval times, most people so wanted to believe in such a kingdom—and in a living unicorn—that they accepted the Prester John letter without investigating its source.

American Unicorns

The same was true for reports that there were unicorns in America. After the New World was discovered in the fifteenth century, stories spread throughout Europe about the wondrous things that could be found there. Unicorns of various kinds were featured in some of these stories. For instance, in 1539 Friar Marcus of Nizza, who accompanied Spanish explorers venturing north from Mexico, wrote in his journal that he had seen "a hide half as big again as that of an ox and told it was the skin of a beast which had but one horn upon its forehead, bending towards its breast, and that out of the same goeth a point forward with which he breaks any thing he runs against."[60]

Furthermore, in 1564 explorer Sir John Hawkins reported seeing unicorns in what is now Florida, and in 1673 a Dutch scientist, Olfert Dappert, wrote in his book "Unbekante Neue Welt" ("Unknown New World"), "On the Canadian border there are sometimes seen animals resembling horses but with cloven hooves, rough manes, a long straight horn upon the forehead, a curled tail like that of the wild boar, black eyes and a neck like that of the stag."[61]

Even after the American continent was fully explored and it was clear that there were no unicorns there, most people continued to accept unicorn reports as true. For example, many people believed British explorer W. Winwood Reade when, in his 1864 book *Savage Africa,* he told of several sightings of wild unicorns in several parts of Africa. Reade described these creatures as being very much like Spanish horses except for the horns on their foreheads.

Looking into the Past

As explorers traveled farther and farther throughout all parts of the world and still brought no unicorns back to civilization, some people decided that unicorns were strictly mythological figures.

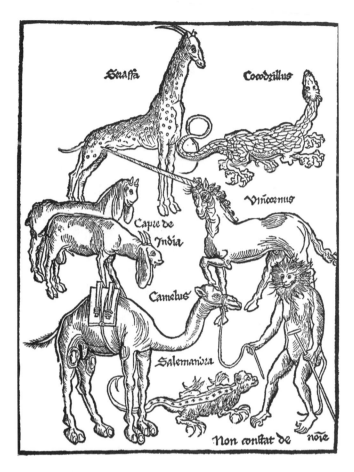

This fifteenth-century sketch shows various exotic animals, one of which is a unicorn.

Others, however, began to look in another place for unicorns: the past. These people argued that unicorns had to have existed at one time—perhaps in prehistoric days—since so many scholars have written about them. Otherwise, as Charles Gould says in his 1886 book *Mythical Monsters*, why did these scholars choose to write about unicorns rather than "start stories of two-legged cows or horses, or one-legged races of men"?[62]

The idea that unicorns were indeed living animals at some time in history was bolstered in the seventeenth century by several discoveries of what appeared to be unicorn fossils. One of the first was discovered in 1663 in a limestone cave near Quedlinburg, Germany. The town was close to the Harz Mountains, where an old legend told of a woman who rode on a unicorn. Therefore, many people believed the discovery was no hoax. They flocked to the cave in large numbers, damaging the site before anyone took charge of excavating the skeleton from the rock in which it rested. The fossil was damaged still further during the excavation process. Afterward the bones were in pieces and some parts of the animal—including half of its spine—were missing. Its skull, however, was intact and featured a seven-and-a-half-foot-long horn.

Modern scholars have come up with various explanations for fossilized skeletons like the one found in Quedlinburg. Some theorize that these fossils were created by a geologic phenomenon. Sometimes petrified wood fuses with bone during the fossilization process, and

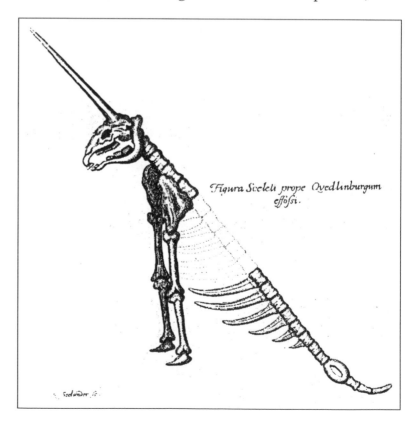

Figura Sceleti prope Qvedlinburgum effossi.

Despite being incomplete, the fossils found at Quedlinburg, Germany, were believed to be those of a unicorn.

experts suggest that this was the case with some of the skulls discovered. In other words, what appeared to be a single horn was actually fossilized wood. Other experts contend that the single horns were natural rock formations like stalactites and stalagmites.

Unicorns in Germany

The Quedlinburg fossil, however, does appear to be of a genuine single-horned animal. Therefore, some modern scholars suggest that it might have come from a long-extinct species of stag or ox—a species that, they speculate, was most likely the unicorn referred to in the Bible.

A few people believe that this unicorn is not extinct but rather continues to live in the remote forest where the fossil was found, a forest so thick that an elusive animal could avoid discovery there. Austrian naturalist Antal Festetics is one such person. In 1991 he reported that while filming a documentary in the Harz Mountains, he saw a unicorn. According to Festetics, "Suddenly a Unicorn came towards me at a gallop. There was a glow of light around the animal. . . . Then, just as quickly, it was gone."[63] Festetics claimed to have captured this image on video and turned the tape over to experts at Gottingen University, where anyone can view it.

In discussing Festetics's sighting in *The Book of the Unicorn*, Nigel Suckling says that it would be possible for a living unicorn to dwell in the forests of the Harz Mountains, calling the place "one of the last true wildernesses left in Europe, a slice of the dark enchanted wood of German folklore and legend, and one of the last possible refuges for creatures such as Unicorns that are unable to tolerate close proximity to humans."[64]

Artificial Unicorns

Suckling's belief that an animal species could remain unknown to humans for so many centuries is not far-fetched. Many new species of animals are discovered by scientists each year in wilderness areas, particularly in thick forests. Thus, some people argue that scientists might one day find a living unicorn as well. Moreover, they point out that the existence of such a creature is not impossible because human beings have been able to create unicorns through artificial means.

There is evidence that man-made unicorns existed in ancient times. They are mentioned in the writings of several scholars, including the Roman naturalist Pliny the Elder. Pliny reported that one ancient method for creating an artificial unicorn involved manipulating the two horns of a young ram or bull on a daily basis so that the horns grew together. Horns are pliable as they grow, and by constant attention they could, according to Pliny, be made to twist around each other.

The horn that resulted from this process would have looked strikingly like a narwhal's tusk—that is, like two long strands that had been twisted into one but formed a straight line from base to tip. This might explain why alicorns were described by the ancients as being twisted or spiraled, even though there is no evidence that narwhal tusks were familiar to the ancient Greeks or Romans.

Another ancient method for making two-horned animals into one-horned animals involves burning a young animal's scalp before the horns' emergence. By scorching the area where horns would appear, the horns would supposedly be redirected to grow out of the center of the skull instead of on the sides. Modern scientists believe that any horns produced by this method would not have appeared healthy. Nonetheless, these horns might have been similar to some of the horns associated with fossilized unicorn discoveries.

In addition to ancient writings, there are stories of tribal cultures in Tibet, Nepal, Mongolia, and Africa that turned two-horned rams or bulls into one-horned ones in order to mark animals that were capable of siring offspring.

This might explain why so many unicorn reports throughout history have come from Asia and Africa. There is also modern proof that the Nepalese knew how to create unicorns. In 1906 the ruler of Nepal gave England's Prince of Wales several one-horned sheep as a present. They were placed on exhibit at the London Zoological Gardens, and at first the English thought they were a rare breed of sheep. But in response to inquiries, a British diplomat who had lived in Nepal reported,

> There is no special breed of one-horned sheep in Nepal, nor are the specimens which have been brought here for sale freaks. By certain maltreatment ordinary two-horned sheep are converted. . . . I am told that the object of producing these curiosities is to obtain fancy prices for them from the wealthy people of Nepal.[65]

Experts who subsequently studied the Nepalese sheep agreed that they were artificially created because the single horn appeared to have two horn buds at its base beneath the scalp, not one. However, the horn was clearly not made by twisting two horns together. Consequently, scientists suspected that the Nepalese were using some method as yet unknown in the Western world.

Dove's Experiment

For many years no one could figure out what this method

Researchers now believe that many unicorns were any variety of two-horned animals that had their horns altered in some way.

This photograph shows Lancelot, one of the four unicorns a California couple created from Angora goats.

might be. Then, in 1933, an American biologist, W. Franklin Dove of Maine University, discovered that horn buds start as pieces of tissue that are beneath the scalp but are not attached to the skull. As the animal grows, the horns root themselves into the scalp. Therefore, Dove theorized that prior to this time the horn tissue could be relocated on another part of the skull.

To prove his theory, Dove operated on a day-old male calf, moving its horn buds to the center of its forehead. After shaving the buds to make them fit together more closely, he placed them side by side. As the animal grew, the horns emerged as one.

In the 1980s a California couple, Morning Glory and her husband, Otter G'Zell, used a similar method to create four unicorns out of Angora goats (although Glory and G'Zell refused to confirm that they had relied on Dove's work). The couple sold these animals to the Ringling Brothers and Barnum and Bailey Circus, which, in 1985, put them on display individually, each billed as "the Living Unicorn." Animal-rights activists were outraged over this, arguing that an animal should not be subjected to unnecessary surgery and pain merely for economic gain. In the wake of bad publicity, Ringling Brothers stopped displaying the animals, but the two Californians continued to produce unicorns for many years.

A Gentle Creation

Interestingly, the artificial unicorns produced by Dove and others have proven to be different in temperament from their two-horned counterparts. They display the same gentle nature that has been mentioned for centuries as being a fundamental characteristic of unicorns. Nigel Suckling believes that this gentleness stems from the fact that a one horned animal has an advantage in a fight with a two-horned animal:

> Dr. Dove's Unicorn bull became the leader of its herd and was very rarely challenged by other males. When bulls charge each other the main aim is to crack skulls until one or other can take no more. Charging towards an enemy who has a spike aimed right between your eyes is a different game altogether. . . . An interesting side effect of the experiment was the nature of the bull's temperament. Being secure in his strength led him to become unusually gentle and mild mannered, echoing what has so often been said of the true Unicorn nature.[66]

Suckling suggests that gentleness is a direct result of having one horn instead of two, regardless of how that horn is created. But some people believe that the gentleness of Dove's unicorns is proof that natural unicorns once existed on Earth. How else, these people wonder, would everyone who wrote about a unicorn have known that a one-horned animal has a gentle nature?

But skeptics point out that there has never been any proof that unicorns—other than man-made ones—ever existed on Earth. Consequently, they believe that all unicorn stories are based on rumor or legend, and they suggest that the ancients who described gentle unicorns could have been applying what they knew about artificial unicorns to the stories they made up about natural ones. Yet if it is true

The question remains whether unicorns were real creatures or merely myths.

that there has never lived a naturally occurring unicorn, why would unicorn stories have endured and remained fairly constant throughout the centuries? As scholar Matti Megged says, "It is still difficult to answer the question of how and why both this enigmatic creature and persistent myth were born and kept alive through thousands of years and countless transformations."[67]

Megged believes that the unicorn is only a myth, born of pure imagination. But this position leaves him—and many others who share his belief—dissatisfied because it presents a mystery as great as whether unicorns were ever real. As Megged asks, "Why, and to what purpose, did all those who created the myth [of the unicorn] need the unique, one-horned creature in order to realize their imaginations?"[68]

Notes

Introduction: An Enduring Figure

1. Nigel Suckling, *The Book of the Unicorn*. Woodstock, NY: Overlook, 1996, p. 128.

Chapter One: What Is the Unicorn?

2. Quoted in Odell Shepard, *The Lore of the Unicorn*. New York: Dover, 1993, p. 37.
3. Quoted in Charles Gould, *Mythical Monsters*. London: W. H. Allen, 1886, pp. 340–41.
4. Ctesias, *Ancient India: As Described by Ktêsias the Knidian*, trans. J. W. McCrindle. Delhi, India: Manohar Reprintings, 1973, p. 26.
5. Joe Nigg, *Wonder Beasts: Tales and Lore of the Phoenix, the Griffin, the Unicorn, and the Dragon*. Englewood, CO: Libraries Unlimited, 1995, p. 76.
6. Philostratus, *The Life of Apollonius of Tyana: On the Existence of Unicorns*, Mountain Man Graphics, 1995. www.magna.com.au/~prfbrown/atyana23.html.
7. Marco Polo, *The Travels of Marco Polo*, trans. Sir Henry Yule, ed. Henri Cordier. New York: Dover, 1993, p. 285.
8. Quoted in Matti Megged, *The Animal That Never Was*. New York: Lumen Books, 1992, p. 8.
9. Quoted in Joe Nigg, *Wonder Beasts*, p. 82.
10. Quoted in Gould, *Mythical Monsters*, pp. 340-41.
11. Ctesias, *Ancient India*, p. 26.

12. Quoted in James Cross Giblin, *The Truth About Unicorns*. New York: HarperCollins, 1991, p. 49.
13. Shepard, *The Lore of the Unicorn*, p. 28.
14. Shepard, *The Lore of the Unicorn*, p. 67.

Chapter Two: A Symbolic Beast

15. Quoted in Megged, *The Animal That Never Was*, p. 5.
16. Shepard, *The Lore of the Unicorn*, p. 94.
17. Elizabeth Pool, *The Unicorn Was There*. Barre, MA: Barre, 1966, p. 7.
18. Pool, *The Unicorn Was There*, p. 10.
19. Pool, *The Unicorn Was There*, p. 44.
20. Shepard, *The Lore of the Unicorn*, pp. 73–74.
21. Shepard, *The Lore of the Unicorn*, p. 73.
22. Megged, *The Animal That Never Was*, p. 18.
23. Quoted in Megged, *The Animal That Never Was*, p. 31.
24. William Shakespeare, *The Tempest*, act 3, scene 3, lines 21–22.
25. Quoted in Shepard, *The Lore of the Unicorn*, p. 84.
26. Megged, *The Animal That Never Was*, pp. 31-32.
27. Megged, *The Animal That Never Was*, p. 27.

Chapter Three: Unicorns and Religion

28. Quoted in Shepard, *The Lore of the Unicorn*, p. 235.
29. Shepard, *The Lore of the Unicorn*, p. 234.

30. Shepard, *The Lore of the Unicorn*, p. 235.

31. Quoted in Suckling, *The Book of the Unicorn*, p. 107.

32. Quoted in Shepard, *The Lore of the Unicorn*, p. 51.

33. Quoted in Megged, *The Animal That Never Was*, pp. 51–52.

34. Quoted in Megged, *The Animal That Never Was*, pp. 64–65.

35. Quoted in Megged, *The Animal That Never Was*, p. 60.

36. Megged, *The Animal That Never Was*, p. 63.

37. Roy Wilkinson, *Are You a Unicorn? The Mission and Meaning of Unicorns.* Kaysville, UT: Unicorns United, 1998, pp. 90–91.

38. Wilkinson, *Are You a Unicorn?* p. 92.

Chapter Four: Magic and Medicine

39. Shepard, *The Lore of the Unicorn*, p. 55.

40. Shepard, *The Lore of the Unicorn*, p. 55.

41. Quoted in Shepard, *The Lore of the Unicorn*, p. 27.

42. Pool, *The Unicorn Was There*, p. 33.

43. Quoted in Shepard, *The Lore of the Unicorn*, p. 35.

44. Quoted in Shepard, *The Lore of the Unicorn*, p. 106.

45. Quoted in Shepard, *The Lore of the Unicorn*, p. 106.

46. Shepard, *The Lore of the Unicorn*, p. 119.

47. Quoted in Joseph Nigg, *The Book of Fabulous Beasts: A Treasury of Writings from Ancient Times to the Present.* New York and Oxford: Oxford University Press, 1999, p. 86.

48. Quoted in Nigg, *The Book of Fabulous Beasts*, p. 86.

49. Quoted in Shepard, *The Lore of the Unicorn*, p. 119.

50. Quoted in Shepard, *The Lore of the Unicorn*, p. 117.

51. Quoted in Nigg, *The Book of Fabulous Beasts*, p. 267.

52. Quoted in Nigg, *The Book of Fabulous Beasts*, p. 267.

53. Shepard, *The Lore of the Unicorn*, pp. 114–15.

Chapter Five: Searching for a Real Unicorn

54. Gould, *Mythical Monsters*, p. 364.

55. Quoted in Shepard, *The Lore of the Unicorn*, p. 259.

56. Quoted in Shepard, *The Lore of the Unicorn*, p. 269.

57. Quoted in Shepard, *The Lore of the Unicorn*, p. 68.

58. Quoted in Shepard, *The Lore of the Unicorn*, p. 195.

59. Quoted in Nigg, *The Book of Fabulous Beasts*, p. 181.

60. Quoted in Suckling, *The Book of the Unicorn*, p. 83.

61. Quoted in Suckling, *The Book of the Unicorn*, p. 83.

62. Gould, *Mythical Monsters*, p. 364.

63. Quoted in Suckling, *The Book of the Unicorn*, p. 66.

64. Suckling, *The Book of the Unicorn*, p. 66.

65. Quoted in Suckling, *The Book of the Unicorn*, p. 86.

66. Suckling, *The Book of the Unicorn*, p. 87.

67. Megged, *The Animal That Never Was*, pp. 159-60.

68. Megged, *The Animal That Never Was*, pp. 159-60.

For Further Reading

Books

Ted Andrews, *Treasures of the Unicorn: The Return to the Sacred Quest*. Batavia, OH: Dragonhawk, 1996. Andrews examines the history and myth of the unicorn, paying particular attention to its healing and magical qualities.

Michael Green, *The Book of the Dragon's Tooth: An Ancient Manuscript on the Secret History of the Dragon and the Unicorn*. Philadelphia: Running, 1996. This beautifully illustrated book is a sequel to *Unicornis*.

———*Unicornis: On the History and Truth of the Unicorn*. 2nd ed. Philadelphia: Running, 1988. This beautifully illustrated book presents information about the unicorn of legends as though it were a real beast.

Paul and Karin Johnsgard, *A Natural History: Dragons and Unicorns*. New York: St. Martin's, 1982. This book offers "factual" information about living unicorns as though they were real, giving details about size, weight, behavior, and habitat in a pseudoscientific fashion. At the same time, it presents information about the symbol and mythological interpretations of the unicorn.

Websites

CKV's Unicorn Page (http://stud-www.uni-marburg.de/~Vigier/uni-main1.html). This website offers basic information about unicorns, but more importantly, it offers links to many other unicorn-related websites.

The Unicorns Meadow (www.geocities.com/Area51/Corridor/4378). This website includes sections entitled "The Legend of the Unicorn" and "The Magic of the Unicorn," and it offers detailed information about the unicorn in history, art, and literature.

Works Consulted

Ctesias, *Ancient India: As Described by Ktêsias the Knidian*. Trans. J. W. McCrindle. Delhi, India: Manohar Reprintings, 1973. The ancient Greek physician Ctesias writes about his adventures in the East.

James Cross Giblin, *The Truth About Unicorns*. New York: HarperCollins, 1991. This little book summarizes basic information about unicorns.

Charles Gould, *Mythical Monsters*. London: W. H. Allen, 1886. In discussing various mythological creatures, Gould argues that the unicorn had to have been a real animal at some point in history.

Matti Megged, *The Animal That Never Was*. New York: Lumen Books, 1992. Megged discusses the unicorn's importance as a mythological and symbolic creature in art and literature.

Joe Nigg, *Wonder Beasts: Tales and Lore of the Phoenix, the Griffin, the Unicorn, and the Dragon*. Englewood, CO: Libraries Unlimited, 1995. Nigg summarizes basic information about the unicorn and provides excerpts from various writings about the animal.

Joseph Nigg, ed., *The Book of Fabulous Beasts: A Treasury of Writings from Ancient Times to the Present*. New York and Oxford: Oxford University Press, 1999. Nigg presents a variety of writings about ancient beasts, including the unicorn.

Marco Polo, *The Travels of Marco Polo*. Trans. Sir Henry Yule. Ed. Henri Cordier. New York: Dover, 1993. The thirteenth-century Italian explorer Marco Polo tells of his travels throughout the Orient.

Elizabeth Pool, *The Unicorn Was There*. Barre, MA: Barre, 1966. This slim volume discusses the myth and meaning of the unicorn.

Odell Shepard, *The Lore of the Unicorn*. New York: Dover, 1993. To date, this is considered the most comprehensive work on the unicorn ever written.

Nigel Suckling, *The Book of the Unicorn*. Woodstock, NY: Overlook, 1996. Suckling summarizes the history of the unicorn in art and literature and relates Eastern and Western legends about its existence and nature.

Roy Wilkinson, *Are You a Unicorn? The Mission and Meaning of Unicorns*. Kaysville, UT: Unicorns United, 1998. Wilkinson argues that the spirit of the unicorn is real and still among human beings.

Internet Source

Philostratus, *The Life of Apollonius of Tyana: On the Existence of Unicorns*, Mountain Man Graphics, www.magna.com.au/ ~ prfbrown/atyana23.html.

Index

Picture Credits

Cover photo: Photo Researchers, Inc.
AP/Wide World, 84
Art Resource, 9, 12, 34
Archive Photos, 50
Corbis, 23, 42, 70
Corbis/Paul Almsay, 57
Corbis/Angelo Harnak, 32, 62
Corbis/Lindsay Hebberd, 38
Corbis/Arnaldo de Luca, 21
Corbis/Francis G. Mayer, 37, 51
Corbis/Francoise de Mulder, 30
Corbis/John Noble, 44
Fortean Picture Library, 8, 47, 52, 55, 60, 65, 68, 73, 75, 80, 83, 86
Library of Congress, 14, 67
Pierpont Morgan Library, 28, 45
Prints Old & Rare, 18
Stock Montage, 13, 17, 26, 76, 79

About the Author

Patricia D. Netzley received a bachelor's degree in English from the University of California at Los Angeles (UCLA). After graduation she worked as an editor at the UCLA Medical Center, where she produced hundreds of medical articles, speeches, and pamphlets. Her books for Lucent's Mystery Library series include *UFOs, The Curse of King Tut, Witches,* and *Haunted Houses.* Her hobbies are weaving, knitting, and needlework. She and her husband, Raymond, live in southern California with their children, Matthew, Sarah, and Jacob.